Crafty Creations

Makes by Susan Hunter-Jones and Katy Rhodes
Photography by Darren Sawyer
Written by Kirsty Neale, Susan Hunter-Jones
and Katy Rhodes
Step art by Dynamo Limited
Spot art by Caroline Martin
Paint effect image from Shutterstock
© Barbaliss
Cover designed by Anisa Asri
Internals designed by Sally Garner
and Clare Phillips

This edition published by Parragon in 2013
Chartist House
15–17 Trim Street
Bath BA1 1HA, UK
www.parragon.com

ISBN 978-1-4723-1165-8

Printed in China

Crafty Creations

Make me!

Make me too!

PaRragon

Bath • New York • Singapore • Hong Kong • Cologne • Delhi
Melbourne • Amsterdam • Johannesburg • Shenzhen

Contents

Welcome to

Crafty Creations

This book is filled with over 100 cool things you can make RIGHT NOW! Whether you feel like painting, drawing, sticking, cutting, stitching, stamping or ripping, there's plenty to keep you busy.

The projects all have simple instructions to follow and helpful photos. It's good to remember that your project doesn't have to look exactly the same as the one in the picture. The instructions are there to guide you, but you can use your own creativity too!

What will I need?

Nearly all the materials you'll need are things you can find around the house. You might want to start collecting some of them now so they'll be ready and waiting the next time you're feeling arty. Find a big box and use it to stash supplies — save up yoghurt pots, keep leftover wrapping paper, ask your parents if you can have old newspapers and don't throw away the stick next time you eat an ice lolly!

Look out for...

You will need:

Some pages start with a list of supplies. Read through it carefully before you get started. If you don't have everything on the list, see if there's something else you can use, or come back to the project another day. There are plenty of others you can do RIGHT NOW instead!

▼ Ask an adult for help with this make.

When you see this, grab yourself a grown-up! It means there's a tricky bit coming up. You'll need an adult to help or to watch and make sure you stay safe.

TiP!

You'll find these handy hints throughout the book. They give suggestions for making things easier or give you extra ideas for projects.

What next?

Read through the next few pages. You'll find a list of materials that could come in handy and some useful techniques. Come back to these at any time — maybe before you start a new project or if you need some extra help along the way. Then...

Ready, steady, MAKE!

Materials

Around the house

Save things from around the house to be ready to make — things from the kitchen, the garden, the bathroom and even your bedroom. Remember to ask permission before you take anything, especially if you're going to paint it, glue it or cut it up!

Cardboard
Coloured paper
Paper towel
Kitchen sponges
Paper plates, bowls, cups
Plastic cups
String
Curly ribbon
Wool
Tinfoil
Foil trays or pans
Paper cake cases
Cotton buds

Straws
Cotton balls
Cotton batting
Tissue paper
Dried food (lentils, beans, etc.)
Seeds, stones, sand, fir cones, leaves, twigs from the garden
Garden stakes
Wooden spoons
Elastic bands
Brown packing paper
Brass fasteners
Bubble wrap

Tip!
Recycle cardboard from packaging, cereal boxes or stiff, board-backed envelopes.

Handy extras

You might already have some of these supplies at home but if not, they're all things you can find in craft shops, and they don't need to cost very much. It's useful to have some of them ready and waiting when you want to get started on a project!

- Ribbon
- Felt
- Sequins
- Gold/silver pens
- Glitter
- Craft feathers
- Buttons
- Beads

TiP!

Cover clothes and work surfaces before you make your crafts, in case anything gets messy!

Crafty tools

Pack these into your arty tool kit and you'll be all set to make just about anything!

- Scissors
- PVA glue
- Glue stick
- Ruler
- Pencil
- Felt-tip pens
- Colouring pencils
- Wax crayons
- Sticky tape
- Double-sided tape
- Masking tape
- Paintbrushes
- Glue spreaders
- Craft paints
- Fabric paint

Recycling and re-using

The things on this page are mostly old, used or unwanted. Some of them might already be on their way to the bin or the recycling pile, but you can save them for makes! Turning rubbish into something new is brilliant fun — it's good for the planet and, best of all, it's free!

Wrapping-paper scraps

Fabric scraps

Sweet wrappers

Buttons

Shells

Beads

Cardboard packaging

Old t-shirts

Old jumpers

Socks

Tights

Gloves/mittens

Ice-lolly sticks

Newspaper

Magazines

Plastic carrier bags

Bottle tops

Yoghurt cups (cleaned out!)

Plastic bottles (large water bottles, small milk bottles)

Cardboard paper-towel rolls

Egg cartons

Glass jars

Old wellies

Mesh bag from potatoes

Old jigsaw-puzzle pieces

Tip!
Don't recycle or re-use anything without checking with an adult first.

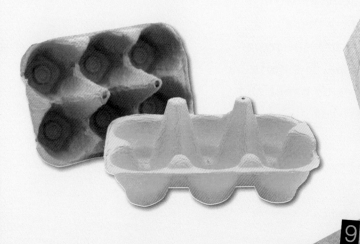

Techniques

Sticky stuff
Different projects need different types of stick!

PVA glue is runny. It's stronger than a glue stick, but it can make thin paper go wrinkly. You can add it to paper, card or fabric with a brush or glue spreader. It dries quite quickly, and is good for sticking card and heavy materials.

A glue stick is solid and dries very quickly. It's good to use on paper projects.

Double-sided tape comes on a roll, like normal sticky tape, but one side is covered with shiny paper. To use it, tear or cut off a piece and press it onto your project. Then peel off the paper backing to show the second sticky side. It's quite strong and is useful for joining pieces of paper and card together without having to wait for glue to dry.

Handy templates

Templates are really useful tracing tools for cutting out exact shapes. They can be simple shapes, like circles and stars, or more complicated designs. Lots of the projects in this book use templates.

You can make most of the easy shapes on your own. Draw them onto card and then cut them out, ready to trace.

For a symmetrical shape, like a heart, fold the card in half first. Draw half the shape against the fold and cut it out. When you unfold and flatten the card again, your template will be perfectly neat and symmetrical!

Tip!

Don't throw templates away when you've finished a project. You might want to use them again! Find an envelope roughly the same size as this book, and fix it to the last page with a paper clip. Slip all your templates inside.

What to use

It's best to make templates from thin card. This makes them easy to cut out but strong enough to trace around.

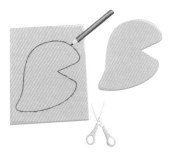

What to do

To use your templates, place them on the back of your paper or fabric. Trace around the edges with a pen or pencil to make an exact copy of the shape. Then cut out!

From the page

To copy shapes you like in this book, grab some tracing paper (or greaseproof paper from the kitchen) and place over the page. Trace the shape in pencil. Remove from the book, then scribble heavily on the back of the paper, filling in the shape. With the scribbled side face down on a piece of card, draw back over the traced shape. Take the paper away to reveal the outline on your card, ready for you to cut out as your template.

Picture perfect

Recycle a plain wooden picture frame, or try cutting your own from cardboard. Give it a fancy new look with these fun decorating ideas.

Back to nature

Place flowers and leaves between sheets of white paper, then squash under a pile of heavy books for two weeks. When they're flat and dry, glue to your frame. Add sticky tape on top to protect the petals.

Or try breaking sticks into pieces, and arrange them on the frame with fir cones. Stick into place with blobs of PVA glue.

Button up

Cover your frame in lots of buttons. Choose a mixture of colours or pick one favourite. Use different sizes and fix them in place with PVA glue.

Puzzle it out

Take the outside pieces from an old jigsaw and paint in different colours. Join them together, then glue to a cardboard frame. For extra sparkle, cover with PVA glue and sprinkle glitter on top.

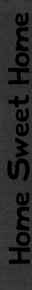

Paper mosaic

Make a mosaic pattern by gluing small squares of paper to a piece of card. Allow to dry, then cut out a heart-shaped frame. Stick a loop of ribbon to the back so you can hang up your finished frame.

! Ask an adult for help with this make.

Twisted tissue

Cut tissue paper into small squares. Fold each square around the end of a pencil, dip into glue and press onto the frame. Stick them as close together as you can for a colourful, scrunchy effect.

Seeds and grains

Stick thin strips of corrugated card sideways along each edge of your frame to make a border. Spread glue over the front of the frame, then sprinkle seeds and grains on top. Glue a ribbon around the outside edge of the frame, leaving a loop for hanging at the top.

It's a sign

1

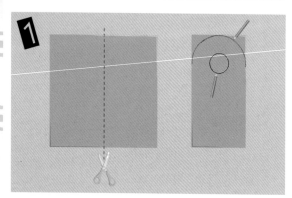

Cut a piece of card to roughly 10 x 20 cm. Trace around a small bowl to make a curve at the top. Draw around an egg cup to mark out a hole in the middle.

2

Cut around the curve at the top. Use a sharp pencil to make a hole in the centre of the circle. Push your scissors through to cut out the circle. Snip 1 cm slots out from the circle.

3

Cut out extra pieces of card to make arms and legs. Stick them into place. Cut out circles to make lights and eyes, and more rectangles for the mouth, teeth, chest and feet. Glue them on to finish off your robot.

TiP!

The slots around the hole are so that your sign will fit around all sorts of doorknobs. You can also adjust the size of the hole if necessary.

TiP!

Add some scraps of tinfoil or use silver card to give your 'bot a cool, metallic look.

Twinkle, twinkle

Start by cutting out a piece of card, just like before, but this time add a curve shape at the bottom too. Draw a moon and some stars onto some card, using felt-tip pens. Cut out each shape and glue to the cardboard sign. Doodle on silver stars and swirls to add some extra sparkle.

Animal crackers

Create a crazy chain of hanging animals by linking up their arms, legs, bodies, trunks or tails!

Dot frogs

The more arms and legs your animals have, the easier they are to join together. These funny frogs are decorated with spots of coloured card glued to their backs.

Slithering snakes

Draw a snake with a curved neck and a loopy tail. Cut out and use as a template to make lots more snakes. Give each one a face and decorate with stripes or triangles of card.

Acro-cats!

To link a line of leaping cats, give each one a curly tail, and carefully cut a little gap between their front paws. You can then hook the tail of each cat through the paws of the one above.

⚠ Ask an adult for help with this make.

Tails and trunks

Elephants have tiny tails, so try hooking their trunks through a loopy back leg instead. Punch a hole and tie on some wool to give each one a perky tail.

Crabby

The bendy legs on these crabs mean you can link them together in lots of different ways. Try it with octopuses and spooky Halloween spiders too.

Tip!

Have a go at mixing up your animals to create a paper zoo! Link a snake to a monkey, then add an elephant or a frog to the chain as well.

Monkey business

Use arms and tails to make a string of cheeky monkeys. Cut their faces from a lighter card colour and draw on eyes, a nose and a mouth with a felt-tip pen.

17

Pots of fun

Give your colouring tools a smart new home with this fun pencil pot!

You will need:

- Cardboard container or can
- Thick paper
- Thin paper (coloured and patterned)
- Scissors
- Double-sided tape
- Glue stick
- Ruler

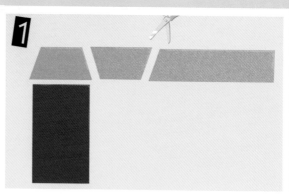

Cut a piece of thick paper the same height as your container and long enough to wrap around it. Cut out coloured paper rectangles to make houses. Use a strip of paper for each roof, cutting the ends off at an angle.

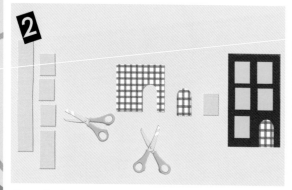

For windows and doors, cut smaller rectangles out of plain or patterned paper. Glue the pieces together to build up each house.

Fix a piece of paper along the bottom of the background strip to look like a road. Stick your houses above it, adding a roof and a paper chimney to each one.

Placing them a little bit lower down, stick another row of houses on top of the first one. Add roofs to each one, but no chimneys.

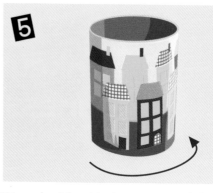

Wrap double-sided tape around the top and bottom edges of the container. Line up your picture and wrap it all the way round. Add extra tape to hold the paper ends in place.

TIP!

Use double-sided tape to stick the houses to the background, so the paper doesn't go crinkly and wrinkly!

TIP!

Try to make each house about half the height of your container.

All at sea

To make a sea-pot for your pencils, cut and stick down wavy strips of blue paper. Cut out a white paper lighthouse and glue red stripes on top. Fix the lighthouse and a tiny paper boat to the waves, before wrapping the paper strip around your container, as before.

Tree mobiles

Hang a string of home-made bugs from your favourite tree!

You will need:

- Thin coloured card
- Pencil
- Glue stick
- Wrapping paper
- Coloured string (or wool)
- Scissors
- Sticky tape
- Sequins

1

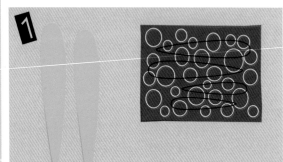

Cut out two dragonfly bodies from coloured card. Draw and cut out two big and two small wing shapes from patterned wrapping paper.

Tip!

If there are no trees in your garden, hang your mobile from a tall plant, balcony or fence instead!

2

Stick the two big wings to the body, near the wide end. Add the small ones just below. Glue the second body on the first so the ends of each wing are hidden in between. Glue on two sparkly sequins as eyes.

3

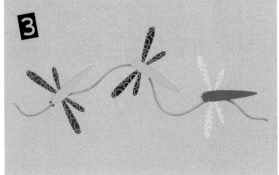

Make more dragonflies in the same way. Tape them to a piece of coloured string or wool and then hang from a tree branch or tall plant.

Tip!

Use plain paper or card if you don't have any gift wrap for the wings. Try adding your own pattern with felt-tip pens or glitter.

Bees in the trees

Decorate another mobile with busy bees and pretty flowers. Cut out a simple flower shape from card and glue on a wrapping-paper centre. To make the bees, start with an oval-shaped body. Add stripes and tiny eyes using a black felt-tip pen, then stick on patterned-paper wings.

21

Tea-light fantastic

Place a small torch inside one of these gorgeous glass holders and watch them glow!

You will need:

- Tissue paper (various colours)
- Scissors
- PVA glue
- Paintbrush
- Ribbon
- Small glass or tea-light holder

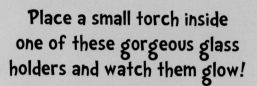

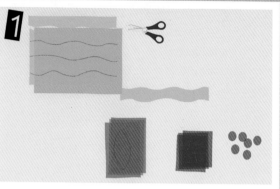

1 Cut blue and green tissue paper into strips with wavy edges. Cut out simple fish shapes in a different colour. Make triangles for their tails and dots for eyes.

2 Brush glue all the way around the bottom half of the glass or holder. Press the tissue strips on top. Overlap the edges, so they look like waves in the sea. Add tissue strips to the top half of the glass in the same way.

3 Leave the glue to dry, then stick on the fish shapes, along with their eyes and tails. Space them out around the glass.

4 Snip off any rough paper edges. Glue a piece of ribbon around the top edge of the glass as a finishing touch.

These holders are not meant for real candles. Instead, stand a small torch or battery-operated tea-light in your glass. Just make sure it isn't raining when you put it outside!

TiP!
Sparkly ribbon looks especially good stuck around the top of your finished glass.

TiP!
Tissue paper is thin, so you can hold a few pieces together and cut through them all at once for quicker snipping!

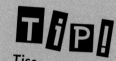

Fold a butterfly

To make a perfect, neat butterfly, fold a piece of tissue in half and cut out a double wing shape against the fold. Open out the paper to reveal your butterfly. Stick to a decorated glass, with a body and some pretty spots on top. Add more butterflies to finish.

Super Socks and fancy streamers

Grab some colourful carrier bags and make one of these brilliant, wind-blown wonders!

Blast off!

Use plastic bags in different colours to cut out two identical rocket shapes, with flames at the bottom. Stick the rockets together at the sides to make a tube. Add a length of thread at the top, then hang your rocket windsock out to flutter in the breeze!

Spooky spider

Draw and cut out a big, dangly spider! Give him eyes, tiny fangs and long legs to blow in the breeze. Make two holes at the top, to tie on your hanging thread.

Tip!

If you're not confident cutting out a rocket shape, draw it on scrap paper first. Cut around your drawing and use it as a template to help you make the plastic version.

Two-colour tube

Cut two rectangles from plastic bags the same length but one twice as wide as the other. Tape the bottom edge of the smaller one to the top edge of the wider one. Snip the wider rectangle into streamers, cutting from the bottom up to the tape. Wrap the smaller rectangle around a piece of cardboard tube and stick in place. Tie thread to the sides of the tube for hanging.

Tip!

Feeling cheeky? Hide your spider in a tree to give your friends a fright!

Crazy zigzags!

Cut out two identical rectangles from a plastic bag and tape the sides together to make a tube. Cut a curve shape at the top, then tie on some thread to make a hanger. Snip the ends of the windsock into strips, giving them zigzag edges.

Fluttering fish

Cut a fish shape from a plastic carrier bag. Stick a strip of double-sided tape along the bottom edge. Cut out long, thin strips from different coloured carrier bags. Press the ends onto the sticky tape. Make a hole at the top of the fish and hang it with a piece of thread.

Tip!

You can cut your streamer strips with straight edges or make them wavy instead.

Windsock it to 'em!

Cut a rectangle shape from a plastic bag and roll it into a tube shape. Stick the edges together with double-sided tape, leaving the bottom two-thirds free. Snip the bottom part into strips all the way around the tube. Tie some thread to the top, to hang your finished windsock out to blow in the wind!

Octo-streamer

Cut out an octopus shape from a carrier bag. Cut out two holes for eyes and stick on streamers in two different colours. Add some beads to the hanging thread for extra fun!

Cupcakes and clowns

Get the party started with these fun and funky invitations!

You will need:

- Thin coloured card
- Pencil
- Scissors
- Paint
- Glue stick
- Ruler
- Felt-tip pens
- Bubble wrap
- Paintbrush
- Coloured paper

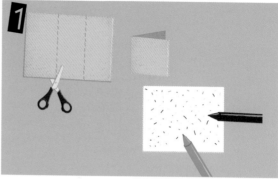

1 For each invitation, cut a piece of card roughly 9 x 21 cm and fold it in half. Decorate another piece of card with felt-tip pens. Draw on lots of dots and dashes to look like sprinkles.

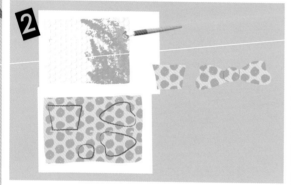

2 Brush paint onto the knobbly side of some bubble wrap. Press it down onto a piece of card to make a dotty pattern, then leave to dry. Cut out a bow-tie shape, a cupcake case and a dot for the clown's hat.

3 Cut out icing for your cupcakes from the sprinkles card. Make extra cupcake layers, some cute cherries, an oval-shaped clown's face, a hat, hair, eyebrows and a mouth from coloured paper.

4 For the clown, glue the hair to your invitation first, then the face, the hat, the eyebrows and the bow-tie. Draw on eyes and cut out a dot from the bubble-wrap card to make a nose. Glue a cupcake on another card in the same way.

Tip!
Add some sparkly swirls to your cupcakes with a gold or silver pen.

Tip!
Mix up the colours and shapes to make all your invitations look a little bit different.

Tip!
You should be able to make three invitations from a single sheet of letter or document-sized card. Try cutting it exactly into thirds so you don't waste a scrap!

27

Take your place

Turn plain plastic or paper cups into the fanciest party place cards!

Party princess

Paint a cup and turn it upside down. Stick on a paper face and arms. Decorate with a button or sequins. Snip a cone of paper into strands to make hair, then trim it so you can see the princess's face. Write your guest's name on a piece of paper, then roll it into a cone-shaped hat. Finish off with curly string.

Good knight

Stick a ball of tinfoil to the bottom of a plastic cup. Cover the whole thing in foil. Make a face, arms, breastplate and shield from paper. Write your guest's name in the middle of the shield and stick it to one of the knight's hands.

Little monsters

Paint a monster onto a cup. Stick on paper arms. To make the flagpole, tightly roll up a piece of paper and glue the edge down. Tape a paper rectangle to the top. Snip out a 'v' shape and add your guest's name. Stick to the monster's hand.

TiP!

Have fun mixing up your paint colours. Remember — monsters come in all different shades!

Cheeky monkey

Try making animal characters instead of paper-cup people. Paint your cup a monkey-ish shade of brown, then add a lighter colour for the face. Draw on eyes, a nose and a mouth, and finish off with some big paper ears.

Feathered friend

Stick a paper beak and wings to a cup that you've painted yellow. Give your chick a pair of googly eyes and stick a fluffy feather to the top of its head.

Cardboard cut-outs

Cut a length of cardboard tube and paint it. Draw a face onto paper and stick to the front of the tube. Glue paper arms to the back, pointing forwards. Snip the edges of a cupcake case into a fringe for hair. Make a flag, as before. Stick to the hand, folding the fingers around the staff.

Tip!

Stir a little bit of PVA glue into your paint if it doesn't seem to be sticking to the plastic cups very well.

Tip!

Paper cups work just as well as plastic ones. Use whichever you can find at home.

29

Hat tricks

Have a go at some simple paper-folding and turn your party guests into Mad Hatters!

You will need:

- Pencil
- Scissors
- Glue stick
- Coloured paper
  (printer or letter-sized plus scraps)

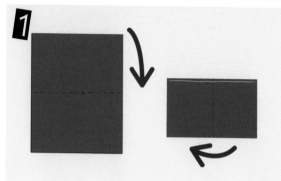

1 Fold a large piece of paper in half widthways. Fold it in half again to make a crease down the middle. Open out the second fold and smooth it flat.

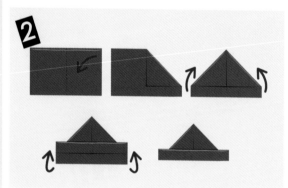

2 Fold the top right corner over so the top edge meets the centre crease. Press firmly along the fold. Do the same on the left-hand side. Fold the front bottom piece upwards. Turn the paper over, and turn the final bottom up.

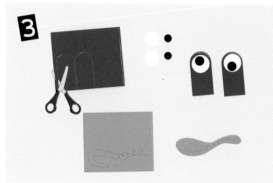

3 Now that you have your basic hat, decorate it! Cut two small arch-shapes the same colour as your hat. Glue black and white circles to the end of each one to make monster eyes. Cut out a wobbly mouth.

4 Stick one eye-stalk to each side of your hat, just behind the diagonal edges. Glue the mouth to the front. Finish off with two small black circles to make a nose.

TiP!

Try folding hats from different types of paper. Leftover gift wrap works brilliantly, and pages from old comics can be fun too.

Paper blossom

For a style that's simple but pretty, cut out a big paper flower and stick it to the brim of your hat.

TiP!

If you prefer, you can stick the eyes right onto the front of the hat, instead of adding eye stalks. Make them big and googly!

Ship shape

How about a hat that looks like a boat? Use scraps of coloured paper to make sails and a flag, then stick on circles for the portholes. All aboard!

Make a mask

Why not give your party a fancy-dress theme and wear one of these amazing masks!

⚠ Ask an adult for help with these makes.

Flower fairy

Draw around a pair of your glasses or sunglasses to make a basic mask template. Copy this onto pink card and cut out. Make eye holes, then decorate the mask with flowers and sparkly sequins. Tape pieces of ribbon or thread to the back of the mask on each side. Tie them together at the back of your head to hold the mask in place.

⚠ TiP!

Draw eyes on your mask, then make a hole in the middle of each one with a sharp pencil. Push scissors through to cut out each of the eye holes.

Mask-o-saurus

Trace around your mask template to make a dinosaur face. Cut out a frill from a different card colour and stick it behind the face. Cut out two horns, a nose and spots to decorate. Glue into position. Make your eye holes using the tip above.

Cool kitty

Using the mask template as a guide, draw the top of a cat's face and cut it out. Stick on triangles inside the ears and a heart for the nose. Add some sequins to each cheek and stick on curly string to make whiskers. Make your eye holes carefully.

Knight time

Draw a pointy knight's helmet around your mask template and cut out. Snip slits for eyes so they look more menacing. Using a different colour, add a nose guard and ear flaps at the sides. Glue buttons across the middle to look like studs.

TIP!

To make the helmet look more like real metal, cut some of the pieces from foil.

Dragon danger

Add big ears to each side of the basic mask outline, then cut out the whole shape. Glue circles of coloured paper over the eyes to make them look bigger. Cut out the eye holes, cutting through both layers. Stick horns to the back of the mask to finish off.

Bird is the word

Cut out a basic mask shape and add a beak near the bottom. Glue a row of feathers along the top of the mask. Decorate with colourful sequins. Make your eye holes carefully.

Beautiful butterfly

Using your mask template as a guide, draw and cut out a butterfly shape. Cut eye holes. Decorate with extra pieces of coloured paper and add sequins or tiny jewels as a fancy, sparkly finishing touch.

Jazzy jewels

Whip up some snazzy jewellery for someone special, or keep it all for yourself!

Tip!

To make a chunkier bracelet, start with 9, 12 or even 15 pieces of wool.

Friendship braids

Cut six pieces of wool, all the same length. Knot together 7-8 cm from one end. Divide into three and start to plait. When the plait is long enough to wrap around your wrist, tie another knot. Cut off the ends, leaving enough spare wool to tie the bracelet in place.

HOW TO PLAIT:

Split your wool or thread into three equal groups. Move the group on the left over the one in the middle and tighten. Then, move the group on the right over the one in the middle and tighten. Do the same again and again until your plait is the right length.

Brilliant beads

Thread beads onto a length of string, ribbon or wool. You can leave gaps between each one or push them more closely together. Tie a knot at each end to hold the beads in place. Leave enough string or ribbon to tie the bracelet around your wrist.

Loopy bangles

Cut loops of kitchen roll tubes with a straight or wavy edge. Paint and leave to dry. Decorate with sequins, ribbon or felt-tip pen drawings. If the kitchen roll is too tight, snip through it so you can easily slide the cardboard bangle on and off your wrist.

Give me a ring

Cut a strip of card big enough to wrap around your finger. Curve it round into a loop shape and stick the ends together. Glue on a button and/or a small shell to decorate.

Bottle-top treasures

Fill an old bottle top with PVA glue. Sprinkle on some glitter or press tiny beads and sequins into the glue. Stick a loop of card to the back to turn it into a ring. To wear it as a brooch instead, fix a piece of double-sided tape to the back.

Tip!

If the double-sided tape isn't sticky enough after you've worn your brooch a few times, just add a new piece on top!

Buttons and bows

Thread a button onto a length of narrow ribbon, and tie a knot. Do the same with another button. Keep going until the button-decorated part of the ribbon is long enough to go around your wrist or neck. Tie the ribbon ends in a bow to hold in place.

Join the band

Cut strips from old socks or pairs of tights. Wear them as colourful wristbands!

In a spin

These spinning tops are easy to make and wheely-good fun, too!

Pie, please!

Cut out two circles of card in different colours. Cut one of them into eight equal-sized sections (like a pie). Glue four of the sections onto the other circle so you have alternating colours. Make a hole in the middle, using a sharp pencil. Push the pencil through the hole. Give the wheel a spin, and watch as the colours mix together to make a new shade!

Spot the difference

Cut out another circle, but this time cover it in spots. You can make your own by cutting them from coloured card, or glue on some spotty wrapping paper.

Tip!

The pencil needs to fit quite tightly through the card circle. If it feels loose, add some glue to hold it in place.

Loop-the-loop

Make two small holes in the middle of a patterned circle with a needle. Use the needle to push a length of thread in through one hole and back out through the other. Knot the ends together so you have a big loop of thread. To use, hold one end of the loop in each hand, with the circle in the middle. Gently pull in and out to watch the wheel spin.

Tip!

If you haven't got any colourful card or wrapping paper, use felt-tip pens to draw your own patterns onto plain paper.

Dizzy frog

Why not cut out a face instead of a circle? Stick on eyes, a mouth and some coloured spots to decorate. Now, see what happens when you give it a spin!

The cat's whiskers

Draw a cat and cut it out. Add some colourful stripes, a mouth and a nose. Glue on eyes and ears or see what happens if you cut those parts out instead.

Gift tags

Make your presents even more special by adding a cool handmade gift tag!

Cutting corners

Cut a rectangle shape out of card and snip each corner into a nice smooth curve. Stick on scraps of paper and fabric to decorate. Punch a hole at one side and use a narrow strip of paper as a tie.

TiP!

Use felt, coloured paper and googly eyes to make a fun picture on the front of your tag.

Brown paper package tags

Glue some brown paper to a piece of card. Cut out a label shape and decorate it however you like. Punch a hole at the top. Thread a length of string through the hole to make a tie.

I love photos

Show someone you really love them with a heart-shaped tag. Cut out the heart from card and punch a hole near the top. Stick on your favourite photograph or cut out a picture from an old magazine instead. Finish off with a ribbon tie or bow.

TiP!

Make sure you ask an adult before you cut up photographs.

38

Big shape, little shape

Simple shapes, such as circles and triangles, make brilliant tags. Decorate them with smaller shapes in different colours. Tie on some smart checked ribbon for the perfect finishing touch.

Make it match!

Make a tag to match the wrapping paper you've used. You can cut out all sorts of different shapes, including butterflies, planes and teddy bears. To turn them into tags, just punch a hole and thread on a tie. Add some extra decoration with buttons, beads or sequins.

Funky flowers

Draw and cut out a flower from card. Glue on a button to make a flower centre. Punch a hole in one of the petals and tie on a piece of curly string.

Prints and patterns

Cut a shape from a piece of sponge and dip it in paint. Press onto a piece of card to make a print. Leave the paint to dry, then cut out a tag around the shape. To make a pattern of circles, try stamping with the end of a pen or pencil instead.

Tip!

Pick a button in a different colour so it stands out.

Fingerprints and flowers

Use dried leaves, flowers and your own fingers to make a bug-tastic scene!

Fly away home

Dip your finger into red paint and press it down flat near your tree. Try to make a nice oval-shaped fingerprint. Leave the paint to dry. Then use a black felt-tip pen to turn it into a ladybird, with legs, antennae and spots.

Start with a tree!

Draw a tree onto brown paper and cut it out. Stick to a plain paper background. Glue dried leaves around the tree branches to decorate.

Blooming marvellous

Snip spiky grass from green paper. Glue along the bottom of the page. Add pressed flowers to some of the stalks. Dip the end of your finger in paint and press gently onto the paper a few times to make tiny fingerprint flowers.

Tip!

To make dried leaves and pressed flowers, pick them from the garden and place onto plain white paper. Place another piece of paper on top. Then add a pile of books or a heavy box. Leave for at least a week. Take them out very carefully, as they will now be fragile.

Tip!

To make round fingerprints use the very tip of your finger. To make oval prints press the top of your finger flat.

Busy bees

Use yellow paint to make some more oval-shaped fingerprints. Allow to dry. Then add smaller fingerprints in light blue to look like wings. Finish off with black felt-tip pen eyes and stripes.

Spider pals

Add some black fingerprints, making them round instead of oval. When the paint is dry, draw on eight black legs. Use tiny dots of white paint to make eyes.

Green bugs

Make some green fingerprints. When they're dry, draw legs and details on top with a felt-tip pen.

TiP!

Dot the white paint on with the end of a cocktail stick.

41

Finger-puppet fun

Keep your fingers busy making these cute puppets!

TIP!

Give each of your finger puppets different faces. They could be happy, sad, worried, surprised, giggly, shout-y or even toothy!

Funny face

Wrap a strip of paper about 7 cm tall around your finger. Overlap the edges, then stick in place to make a tiny tube. Cut a pair of arms from card and glue to the sides. Stick some wool at the top to make hair. Draw on a mouth in felt-tip pen and finish off with two googly eyes.

Paper people

Make a finger tube from paper, as before. Cut out a circle of card and draw a face on one side. Stick it to the top of your tube. Decorate with extra pieces of card. Use wool to make hair. Glue buttons or sequins to the tube.

Sheep-shape!

Cut two arch-shaped pieces of white felt, big enough to fit over your finger. Glue or stitch them together, leaving the bottom open. Draw a sheep's head onto felt and cut out. Use a black felt-tip pen to draw on a face. Glue the head to the top of the body.

TIP!

Stick a photo of a person or an animal to the top of the tube instead of drawing the face.

Puppy love

Make a light-brown felt body, gluing or stitching two arches together. Cut out a dog's head, ear and round snout in the same colour. Cut an ear and eye patch from dark brown felt and a nose from black felt. Glue the pieces together, then stick the head to the body and draw a mouth.

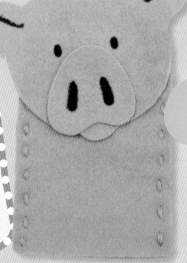

Oink!

Cut a pig's head and cute snout from pink felt. Glue them together and draw on a face with a felt-tip pen. Cut out and stitch a pink felt finger-puppet body. Glue the head and body together.

T!P!

Use face paints to turn your fingers green so they match the dragon's body!

! Ask an adult for help with this make.

! Ask an adult for help with this make.

Tiny dragon

Draw the top part of a dragon onto card and colour it in. Cut out, then make two holes near the bottom edge. Push your fingers through the holes to make the dragon's legs. Wiggle them around to make him walk, run or do something silly, such as dance ballet.

Sir Finger-legs

Draw the head, body and shield of a knight onto card. Colour it in and cut out. Make holes at the bottom for your fingers, as for the dragon.

Cool for caterpillars

Make some woolly pom-poms, then turn them into a mountain of mini-beasts!

You will need:

- Thick card
- Scissors
- Large needle
- Felt (black and white)
- Ruler
- Wool (three colours)
- PVA glue

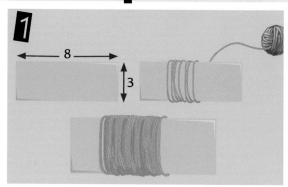

1 Cut a 3 x 8 cm piece of thick card. Wind your wool around it widthways about 40 times. Don't wind too tightly! Snip the end of the wool strand and carefully slide the whole wool bundle off the card.

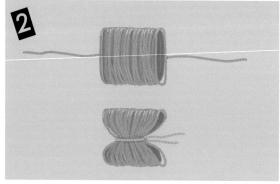

2 Place the bundle down on top of a long piece of wool. Tie the wool tightly around the middle of the bundle in a double knot.

3 Cut through the loops on both sides of the bundle to make a pom-pom. Fluff it up with your hands and snip off any straggly ends. Make seven more pom-poms in the same way, using three different colours of wool.

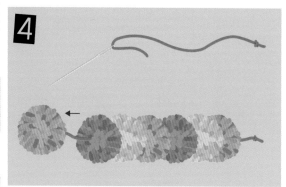

4 Thread a length of wool onto a needle and knot the end. Push the needle through the tied area in the middle of each pom-pom. Tie a knot to hold the line of pom-poms in place. Snip off the leftover wool.

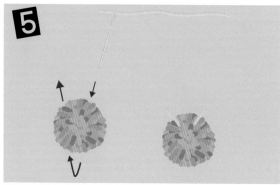

5 To make antennae, sew a piece of wool down through the head and back up on the other side. Snip the ends so they're the same length. Cut eyes and a mouth from felt. Stick to the head with PVA glue.

Green and greener

For a multi-coloured pom-pom, wind two different wool colours around the card at the same time.

Tip!

Ask a friend to put their finger on the first knot when you're tying the wool bundle together. It will hold everything in place and make it easier to tie the second part of the knot.

Pom-pom python

Make more pom-poms and thread them together to create a slippery snake. Leave each pom-pom flat instead of fluffing it up so the snake has thinner stripes than the caterpillar. Finish off with a forked tongue cut from felt.

What's the buzz?

It only takes three pom-poms to whip up a busy bee! Sew on two loops of white wool to look like tiny wings.

Monster mayhem

What's even scarier than stinky old socks? A sock monster, of course!

You will need:

- Old sock
- Scissors
- Thin card
- Cotton-wool balls
- Masking tape (optional)
- Pencil
- PVA glue
- Glue spreader

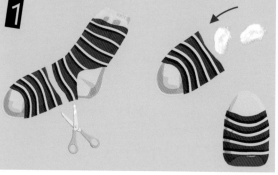

1 Cut off the foot of your sock, just below the heel. Stuff the toe part with cotton-wool balls. Fold over the ends of the sock and glue them together.

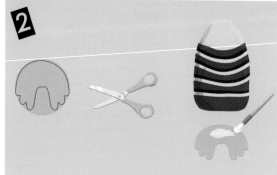

2 Cut a circle out of card, the same width as your stuffed sock. Snip away the front of the circle to make a pair of feet. Spread glue over the back of the feet. Press the stuffed sock down on top. Leave to dry.

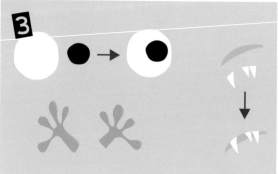

3 Cut eyes, a mouth and pointy teeth from card. Glue a black pupil to each white eye and stick the teeth on the mouth. Cut arms from the same card colour as the legs.

4 Stick each card piece to the sock with PVA glue. If you wish, use masking tape to hold them in place while the glue dries.

Best foot forward

Uh-oh, that sock's escaping! To give your rabbit (or monster) walking feet, cut two oval shapes from card. Stick one under the body to make the normal, flat foot. Stick the other under the body, sticking out enough to fold the front upwards at an angle to make the bunny walk!

TIP!

It doesn't matter if your stuffed sock is lumpy — this will just make it look even more monster-ish!

Funny bunny

To make a sock rabbit, cut the feet, arms, ears and nose from felt. Glue them on, as before. Add felt or button eyes, some wool for whiskers and a cotton-wool ball as a tail!

TIP!

For an even crazier look, give your monster giant googly eyes or make one eye bigger than the other! Try cutting feet and hands in different shapes and sizes, too.

Monster measles

Cut circles from brightly coloured card and glue them all over your sock to make a spotty monster. Turn him into a Cyclops by sticking on one eye instead of two.

47

Top of the pops

Simply snip, fold and stick all these brilliant pop-up cards!

You will need:

- Thin card
- Scissors
- Pencil
- Felt-tip pens
- Paper
- Glue stick
- Sequins (optional)

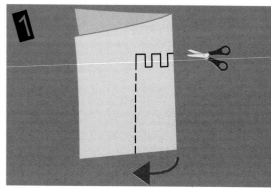

1 Fold a piece of card in half. Just over halfway up the card, cut battlement shapes going in from the folded edge. Open the card and push the tower forwards to form a box. Press down on the creases.

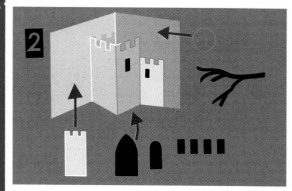

2 Glue another piece of card behind the first. Cut two smaller towers from card. Stick one on each side of the box. Cut windows, doors and branches from black paper and a moon from white paper. Glue into position.

TiP!
Cut out a coloured paper flag to fly over your castle.

TiP!
After cutting it out, push the pop backwards and forwards to make a good crease.

48

Hooting hello

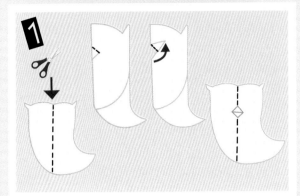

1

Draw an owl shape onto card and cut out. Fold down the middle. To make a beak, snip a small line going diagonally upwards from the fold. Fold at an angle to crease. Open out the card and push the beak forwards.

2

Fold a piece of card in half. With the beak pushed forwards, stick the owl to the card, lining up the centre folds. Draw on feathers and add a paper wing, legs and eyes. Cut out leaves and branches and stick in place.

My heart bursts

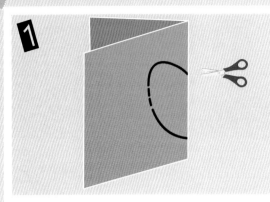

1

Fold your card in two. Draw half a heart against the folded edge. Cut out from both ends, leaving an un-cut section in the middle. Decorate, then push the heart forwards to make it pop. Glue to a piece of folded card.

Tip!

Decorate the card with sequins, paper shapes and a sparkly silver pen.

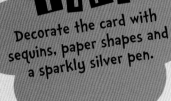

Smart silhouettes

Make paper silhouettes by mixing bright colours with lots of shadowy black.

Did you know?

A silhouette is a bit like a shadow. It's a dark, filled-in outline of a shape against a light background. You often see building silhouettes at night, especially in towns and cities.

Skyscraper style

Rectangles make perfect buildings. They can be long and thin, or small and wide. Cut them out from orange or yellow paper to make windows too.

City skyline

Cut out pieces of paper to make this cool city-scene picture. Use black for the building silhouettes and coloured pieces on top to look like windows and lights. Square shapes are especially good for windows. Stick them on in groups of four to make separate panes of glass.

Round and round

Coloured circles and arches are good for making unusual windows. You could try sticking a black arch or half-circle on top of a rectangle-shaped building too.

Triangle toppers

Cut triangles of black paper and stick over some of the tall buildings. Add thin lines for aerials or church spires.

Bright blue

Office blocks have lots of windows. Cut long strips of coloured paper and stick them down in lines. Use blue instead of orange or yellow for some really sleek city style.

Stained-glass lantern

Cut out a long strip of card and carefully cut shapes out of the middle. Stick pieces of coloured tissue paper behind the shapes to make a stained-glass effect. Curve the card round and glue the ends together. Add a narrow strip of card at the top to make a handle.

 Ask an adult for help with this make.

TIP!

Hang your lantern in a window so sunlight can shine through the tissue paper.

Haunted house

Make a frame from black card. Draw and cut out a spooky castle and a creepy, spiky tree. Glue them inside the frame. Add some purple tissue paper for the night sky. Use yellow or orange tissue behind the doors and windows. Hang the picture in your bedroom window and wait for the full moon to make it glow.

Flying colours

Fold an ordinary piece of paper into one of these plane-ly brilliant flyers!

You will need:

● Letter or printer-sized paper
● Felt-tip pens to decorate (optional)

TiP!

To add cool stripes to your plane, draw felt-tip pen lines onto the paper before you start folding. Use as many colours as you like!

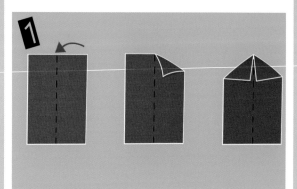

Fold a piece of paper in half and crease. Open it out flat again. Fold the top right corner over diagonally so the top edge lines up with the centre crease. Do the same with the top left corner.

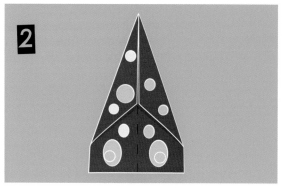

Fold the right-hand side over again. The new corner should meet the centre crease. Repeat on the left-hand side. Decorate.

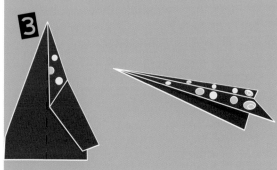

Turn the paper over. Fold both outside edges in to the centre crease. Turn the paper over again. Push the side edges together. Hold the centre fold between your fingers and thumb and open out the sides to become wings.

All fired up

Add some fun flame decorations to make your plane look super smart. Stick them on top of the wings and glue an extra one at the back, in between the centre fold.

Tip!

Press firmly along each fold with your fingers to make neat, strong creases.

On the wing

Is it a bird or is it a plane? It's both! Glue on some circles for eyes and two orange triangles as a beak. Add black dots. Snip the back corners of the plane so they look like feathers.

Tip!

Use thin paper to add decorations to your plane and stick the same number of things on each side to balance it out.

53

Paper shaper

From cats and frogs to witches and wizards, these cute cone characters couldn't be easier to make!

Take bat!

Draw and cut out a semi-circle from black card. Move the corners towards each other, so the paper curves round into a cone shape. Overlap the edges and stick together. Cut a head and wings from black card. Draw a face onto the head in silver pen. Glue the head to the top of the cone and the wings to the back.

Pretty kitty

Make a black cone, as before. Cut out a head, tail and white tummy. Cut out an oval-shaped face, with an extra section of fringe on each side to look like whiskers. Stick this to the head and draw on a face. Add a pink triangle to each ear, then glue the head, tail and tummy pieces to the cone.

Mighty mouse

Tip a brown paper cone sideways and stick a tail to the back. Cut out a pair of ears. Fold over a tab at one end, then glue to the cone and draw on some eyes. Snip white paper into a fringe to make whiskers. Add pink paper to each ear and a pink circle for a nose.

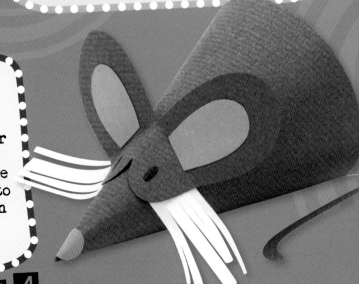

Croak!

Cut out a frog face and stick to the top of a green cone. Add two white circles for eyes. Draw on black pupils, a mouth and nose. Decorate the cone with circles of light green card.

Tip!

Use a clothes peg to hold your cone together as the glue dries.

Tip!

Decorate the witch and wizard with moons and stars!

Which witch?

Make a black cone, then slide a ring of card over it to look like a hat brim. Draw and cut out a face. Snip a fringe into some white paper to make hair. Glue the face and hair to the cone, underneath the hat brim. Stick arms and hands to the sides of the cone.

Abracadabra!

Make a matching wizard from purple card. Glue an extra piece of paper to the back of the cone as a cloak. Stick a paper beard under the face and stick a thin strip of card to one hand to make a wand.

Farmyard friends

Tear up old brown envelopes and yesterday's newspapers to make these feathery farmyard birds.

You will need:

- Coloured paper
- Scissors
- Felt-tip pen
- Old brown envelope
- Old newspaper
- Pencil
- Glue stick

Tip!

You can recycle white envelopes as well as brown ones. Lots of them have really cool patterns printed on the inside. Tear one open and see what you find!

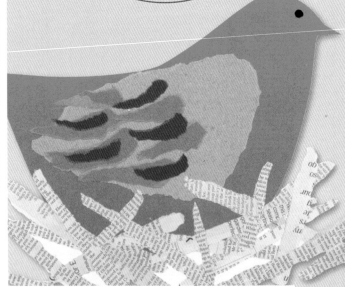

1

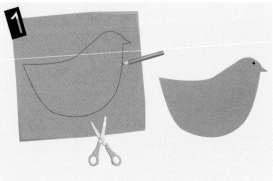

Draw a hen onto paper and cut her out. Add an eye using a black felt-tip pen.

2

Tear a wing shape from an old brown envelope. Tear smaller strips of brown paper to make feathers and small strips of newspaper for straw.

3

Stick the hen onto a white paper background. Glue the wing and feathers on top. Add the strips of newspaper to make her nest.

Owl post

Cut an oval shape from brown paper. Tear out wings, feet, feathers and a face. Glue them to the oval to make a fluffy but wise old owl.

Cock-a-doodle-doo!

Cut and tear paper pieces to make a cockerel. Add a comb to his head and a big, feathery tail.

Bottle-top bugs

Start saving up your bottle lids so you can make these brilliant bugs!

You will need:

- Red or black bottle lid
- Thin card
- Pencil
- PVA glue
- Glue stick
- Scissors
- Felt-tip pen
- Glue spreader

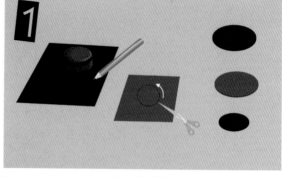

1 Draw around your bottle lid onto black card and again onto red card. Cut out both pieces. Cut a smaller circle of black card for the head.

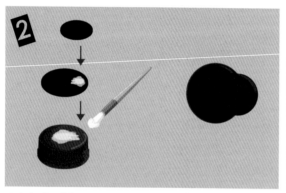

2 Stick the black circle onto the lid. Glue the head on top so it overlaps the edge a little bit.

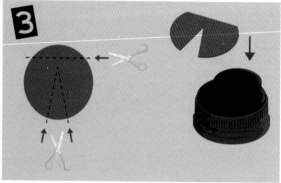

3 Snip a small piece off one side of the red circle. Cut out a triangle on the opposite side to make the wings. Spread glue along the flat edge of the wings. Stick to the lid, just behind the head.

4 Cut out two circles of white card and two smaller black circles. Stick together to make eyes, then glue to the front of the head. Use a felt-tip pen to draw black dots on the wings.

TIP!

If you can't find lids in the right colour for your bugs, have a go at painting a plain white one the colour you want instead.

TIP!

Bend the wings up a little bit at the back. It will make your ladybird look like it's about to fly away home!

Bottle-top bumblebee

Draw felt-tip pen stripes onto yellow card to make a cute bumblebee. Cut petal shapes from white paper to make wings and add small black dots for eyes.

Dragonflies

Make double wings by cutting out four long petals. Use shiny paper for an even prettier bug!

Meet the beetles

To give your bug a smart, patterned body like these beetles, stick a circle of stripy card to the lid. Snip two circles in half to make two sets of wings and add a smaller half-circle on top for the head. Use sequins for eyes.

Box clever

Store your stuff in some of these cool containers - all made from old tins and boxes!

Spongepot star-stamps!

Cut a strip of paper to fit around an empty food container and stick in place. Snip pieces of kitchen sponge into shapes. Dip the shapes into paint and print a pattern onto the container. Leave to dry.

TIP!

Look out for tube-shaped containers that hold things such as crisps or biscuits. They often have lids, which are even more useful for storing your treasures safely inside. Just make sure to clean them out first!

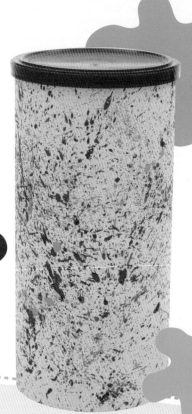

Hex box

Old chocolate boxes are often an interesting shape, like this hexagon. To decorate, cut out pictures from old magazines. Spread glue over the back of each one and press down onto the box. Overlap the edges of the pictures so the box is completely covered.

On your marks, get set, splatter!

Cut a strip of paper to fit around an empty food container and stick in place. Dip a big paintbrush into some paint. Use it to flick and splatter paint all over the paper. Use different colours to create an interesting and bright splatter pattern. Leave to dry.

TIP!

This is a messy project, so spread out some old newspapers under the paper to protect the floor and table. If you can do your paint-splattering outside, that's even better!

Ladybird loot-stasher!

Cover a box with red tissue paper and carefully cut a hole in the top. Cut out a face with two spiky antennae from black card. Make it a little bit bigger than the front of the box. Glue into position and stick on some eyes. Cut legs from black card and glue to the bottom of the box. Decorate with black spots.

⚠ Ask an adult for help with this make.

Tip!

Try making your ladybird from a small tissue box that already has a hole cut in the top.

Moneybox monster

Glue coloured tissue paper all the way around a tall, thin cardboard box. Cut a slot on one side to make a mouth. Stick on arms, eyes and some colourful spots. Drop your pocket money in through the mouth and the monster will keep your savings safe. Just make sure the slot is big enough to get the money out again!

Cereal stripes

Take an empty cereal box and cut off the top. Cover the box in paper. Cut triangle shapes out of the top edge to make a zigzag pattern. Add some smart stripes to the box by sticking on strips of coloured and patterned paper.

Pop-up Pals

Turn a plain yoghurt pot and straw into jolly jumping characters!

You will need:

- Plastic yoghurt pot
- Paint
- Tissue paper
- PVA glue
- Pencil
- Bendy straw
- Paintbrush
- Scissors
- Thin card
- Felt-tip pens
- Sticky tape

! Ask an adult for help with this make.

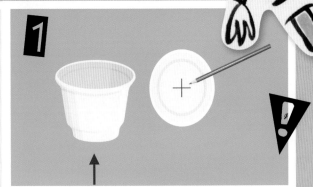

1 Ask an adult to make a hole in the bottom of your yoghurt pot with a craft knife. Get the adult to cut two slits in a cross shape and push a pencil through to make a hole.

2 Paint your yoghurt pot a bright colour. You might need to brush on a few coats to cover up the words and pictures on the pot.

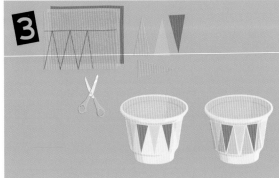

3 Cut out triangles of tissue paper in two or three different colours. Use PVA glue to stick the triangles around the edge of the pot. Do one row facing down and one facing up. Mix up the colours as you go.

4 Draw a clown onto a piece of card. Colour in with felt-tip pens, then cut out. Tape to the straight end of your bendy straw.

5 Push the straw through the hole in your yoghurt pot. This is now the clown's drum! Slide the straw up and down so it looks as though the clown is jumping on the drum.

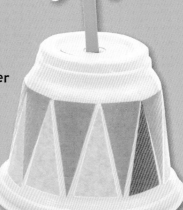

Tip!

Draw some more clowns in different jumping positions!

Tip!

Once you've pushed your straw into the yoghurt pot, bend over the end so it doesn't slide out again.

Tip!

Stick a whole row of tissue triangles down before you add the next one. It's much easier to fit the shapes together this way.

Leap frog

Use your yoghurt pot the other way up to turn it into a pond. Paint it blue inside and green on the outside. Decorate with grass and flowers. Add a cute frog to the end of the straw, then make him leap in and out of the pond.

Little bird

Say hello to a garden visitor who won't fly away, even in winter!

You will need:

- Thin card
- Thin fabric
- Pencil
- Button
- Small brush or glue spreader
- PVA glue
- Scissors
- Felt
- Garden stake

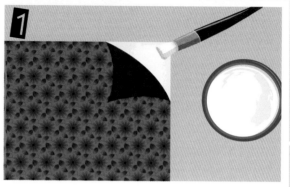

1 Brush glue all over a piece of thin card. Place a piece of fabric on top and smooth it out with your hands to get rid of any creases. Leave this to dry.

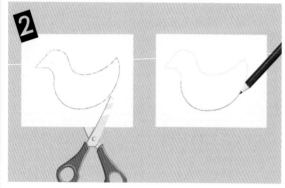

2 Turn the card over so the fabric is facing down. Draw a simple bird on the card and cut it out. Trace the shape onto another piece of card and cut that out too.

3 Take the fabric-covered bird and spread glue around the edges on the card side. Leave a gap at the bottom. Press the second bird down firmly on top. Leave this to dry.

4 Cut a wing and beak from felt. Glue into place and stick on a button eye. Brush some glue around the top of a garden stake. Slide it into the gap at the bottom of the bird. Lay it down flat and leave to dry.

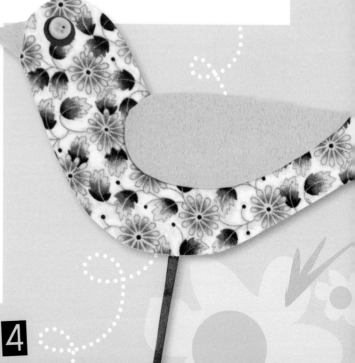